Sound It Out

More Consonants

by Wiley Blevins
illustrated by Sean O'Neill

Red Chair Press   Egremont, Massachusetts

Look! Books are produced and published by Red Chair Press:

Red Chair Press LLC   PO Box 333   South Egremont, MA 01258-0333

www.redchairpress.com

 FREE activity page from www.redchairpress.com/free-activities

Wiley Blevins is an early-reading specialist and author of the best-selling *Phonics from A to Z: A Practical Guide* from Scholastic and *A Fresh Look at Phonics* from Corwin. Wiley has taught elementary school in both the United States and in South America. He has written more than 70 books for children and 15 for teachers, as well as created reading programs for schools in the U.S. and Asia.

Publisher's Cataloging-In-Publication Data

Names: Blevins, Wiley. | O'Neill, Sean, 1968- illustrator.

Title: More consonants / by Wiley Blevins ; illustrated by Sean O'Neill.

Description: Egremont, Massachusetts : Red Chair Press, [2019] | Series: Look! books : Sound it out | Includes word-building examples. | Interest age level: 004-008. | Summary: "The alphabet has 26 letters -- 21 of them are consonants. They can be combined with vowels to build words. Readers discover what some of the less frequent consonants can do."--Provided by publisher.

Identifiers: ISBN 9781634403375 (library hardcover) | ISBN 9781634403498 (paperback) | ISBN 9781634403436 (ebook)

Subjects: LCSH: English language--Consonants--Juvenile literature. | English language--Pronunciation--Juvenile literature. | CYAC: English language--Consonants. | English language--Pronunciation.

Classification: LCC PE1159 .B543 2019 (print) | LCC PE1159 (ebook) | DDC 428.13--dc23

LCCN: 2017963410

Illustrations by Sean O'Neill

Photo credits: iStock

Printed in the United States of America

0918 1P CGBS19

Our alphabet has 26 letters.

5 of these letters are vowels.

A-E-I-O-U

The rest are called **consonants**.

Let's see what these consonants can do.

Table of Contents

Gg

Gulp, gulp, gulp
that grape juice.
Go. Go. Good!

Say the sound for g.
It's the first sound
you hear in <u>good</u>.
Say the sound many
times fast: "g" "g" "g".
G

Game. Girl. Ghost.

Hh

How hot is it in here?
Hand me a fan.
I'll keep it near.

Say the sound for <u>h</u>.
It's the first sound
you hear in <u>hot</u>.
Say the sound many
times fast: "h" "h" "h".
H

Hop. Horse. Hello.

Kk

Kick that ball.
Keep it close, then
kick it in the net!

Say the sound for <u>k</u>.
It's the first and last
sound you hear in <u>kick</u>.
Say the sound many
times fast: "k" "k" "k".
K

King. Kiss. Kangaroo.

Meet the
king of kick.

Jj

Jill jumps jump rope
just like that.
Jump. Jump. Jump.
Jump rope fast.

Say the sound for j. It's the
first sound you hear in <u>jump</u>.
Say the sound many
times fast: "j" "j" "j".
J

Jug. Jet. Jar of jelly.

Ww

Wash that window.
Wash it well.
Wide and deep,
'cause we can tell.

Say the sound for <u>w.</u> It's the first sound you hear in <u>wash</u>. Say the sound many times fast: "w" "w" "w". W

Winter. Water. Wiggle.

13

Vv

Viola plays the violin.
She plays it very, very well.

Say the sound for <u>v</u>.
It's the first sound
you hear in <u>very</u>.
Say the sound many
times fast: "v" "v" "v".
V

Van. Vase. Volcano.

Yy

The yo-yo goes up and down. Yell for more and it will spin around.

Say the sound for y. It's the first sound you hear in yo-yo. Say the sound many times fast: "y" "y" "y". Y

Yak. Yolk. Yellow.

Zz

Zip that zipper. Zzzz.
Zip it fast!

Say the sound for z.
It's the first sound
you hear in zip.
Say the sound many
times fast: "z" "z" "z".
Z

Zebra. Zoo. Zig-zag.

Qq

Q is a special letter. It needs a friend by its side. What friend? The letter u. Together they make the sounds "kw."

Say the sounds for <u>qu</u>. They are the first sounds you hear in <u>quiet</u>. Say the sounds many times fast: "kw" "kw" "kw". Qu

Queen. Quick. Quit.

Xx

Open the box.

The letter x comes at the end of words. It stands for two sounds put together: "ks".

Say the sounds for <u>x</u>. They are the last two sounds you hear in <u>box</u>. Say the sounds many times fast: "ks" "ks" "ks". X

Fox. Fix. Wax.

Let's Build Words

These are some of the consonants.

Let's make words with them.

The consonants plus a vowel are all we need.

Ready, set, read!

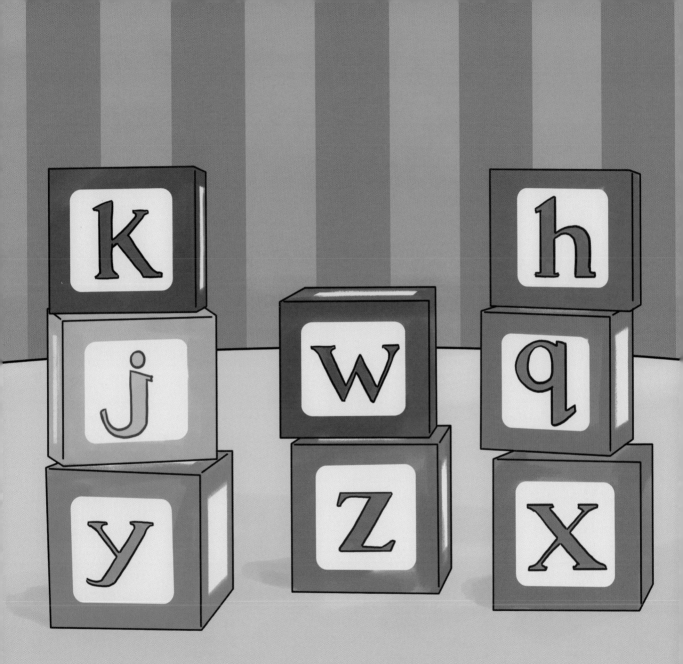

Say the sound for <u>w</u>.
Now say the sound for <u>a</u>.
Put the two together: <u>wa</u>.
Add the sound for g
to the end.

What word did you make?
wag

Wag, wag, wiggle.
The dog's tail can
jiggle, jiggle, jiggle!

Wag and wiggle.

Say the sound for s.

Now say the sound for i.

Put the two together: si.

Add the sounds for x

to the end.

What word did you make?

six

Two plus four.

Or three plus three.

It's all the same,

as you can see.

$$2 + 4 = 6$$

$$3 + 3 = 6$$

$$5 + 1 = 6$$

Say the sound for <u>h</u>.

Now say the sound for <u>a</u>.

Put the two together: <u>ha</u>.

Add the sound for <u>t</u>

to the end.

What word did you make?

hat

Grab a hat. A cap.

A sombrero.

It's time to play in the sun!

Hat. Hot. Hut. Hit.

That's all. This is it!

Our alphabet has 26 letters.
5 of these letters are vowels.

A-E-I-O-U

The rest are called **consonants**.

Now you know what these consonants can do.